MAX on life
:::::::::::::::: cd-book :: study

Gaining a
New Attitude
on Life

:: 4 Interactive Bible Studies
for Individuals or Small Groups

MAX LUCADO

THOMAS NELSON PUBLISHERS

CONTENTS

HOW TO USE
THIS STUDY GUIDE

Congratulations! You are making God's Word a priority. These moments of reflection will change you forever. Here are a few suggestions for you to get the most out of your individual study.

1

As you begin each study, pray that God will speak to you through his Word.

2

Read the overview to each study, then listen to the audio segment, taking notes on the worksheet provided.

3

Following the audio segment, respond to the personal Bible study and reflection questions. These questions are designed to take you deeper into God's Word and help you focus on God and on the theme of the study.

4

There are three types of questions used in the study. *Observation* questions focus on the basic facts: who, what, when, where, and how. *Interpretation* questions delve into the meaning of the passage. *Application* questions help you get practical: discovering the implications of the text for growing in Christ. These three keys will help you unlock the treasures of Scripture.

5

Write your answers to the questions in the spaces provided or in a personal journal. Writing brings clarity and deeper understanding of yourself and of God's Word.

6

Keep a Bible dictionary handy. Use it to look up any unfamiliar words, names, or places.

7

Have fun! Studying God's Word can bring tremendous rewards to your life. Allow the Holy Spirit to illuminate your mind to the amazing applications each study can have in your daily life. ∎

INTRODUCTION

GAINING A NEW ATTITUDE ON LIFE

Once there was a man whose life was one of misery. The days were cloudy, and the nights were long. Henry didn't want to be unhappy, but he was. With the passing of the years, his life had changed. His children were grown. The neighborhood was different. The city seemed harsher.

He was unhappy. He decided to ask his minister what was wrong.

"Am I unhappy for some sin I have committed?"

"Yes, the wise pastor replied. "You have sinned."

"And what might that sin be?"

"Ignorance," came the reply. "The sin of ignorance. One of your neighbors is the Messiah in disguise, and you have not seen him."

The old man left the office stunned. "The Messiah is one of my neighbors?" He began to think who it might be.

Tom the butcher? No, he's too lazy. Mary, my cousin down the street? No, too much pride. Aaron the paperboy? No, too indulgent. The man was confounded. Every person he knew had defects. But one was the Messiah. He began to look for Him.

He began to notice things he hadn't seen. The grocer often carried sacks to the cars of older ladies. *Maybe he is the Messiah.* The officer at the corner always had a smile for the kids. *Could it be?* And the young couple who'd moved next door. *How kind they are to their cat. Maybe one of them . . .*

With time he saw things in people he'd never seen. And with time his outlook began to change. The bounce returned to his step. His eyes took on a friendly sparkle. When others spoke he listened. After all, he might be listening to the Messiah. When anyone asked for help, he responded; after all this might be the Messiah needing assistance.

The change in attitude was so significant that someone asked him why he was so happy. "I don't know," he answered. "All I know is that things changed when I started looking for God."

Let the following lessons start you on the path of looking for God and finding a new attitude. ■

Write today's worries in sand.
Chisel yesterday's victories in stone.

MAX LUCADO

LESSON ONE:

HOW TO GET
OUT OF A SLUMP

*Brothers and sisters, think about the things
that are good and worthy of praise.*

PHILIPPIANS 4:8

OVERVIEW

Two types of thoughts continually vie for your attention. One says, "Yes you can."

The other says, "No you can't." One says, "God will help you." The other lies, "God has left you." One speaks the language of heaven; the other deceives in the vernacular of the Jebusites. One proclaims God's strengths; the other lists your failures. One longs to build you up; the other seeks to tear you down. And here's the great news: you select the voice you hear. Why listen to the mockers? Why heed their voices? Why give ear to pea-brains and scoffers when you can, with the same ear, listen to the voice of God?

Do what David did in 2 Samuel 5:6-9. Turn a deaf ear to old voices. And, as you do, open your eyes to new choices. When everyone else saw walls, David saw tunnels. Others focused on the obvious. David searched for the unusual. Since he did what no one expected, he achieved what no one imagined. Get creative with problem solving.

If the wall is too tall, try a tunnel.

David found fresh hope in a hole outside the Jerusalem walls. So can you. Not far from David's tunnel lies the purported tomb of Christ. What David's tunnel did for him, the tomb of Jesus can do for you. "God's power is very great for us who believe. That power is the same as the great strength

God used to raise Christ from the dead and put him at his right side in the heavenly world" (Eph. 1:19-20).

Do what David did.

Turn a deaf ear to the old voices.

Open a wide eye to the new choices. God loves to give them.

PART 1:
FOLLOW-ALONG NOTES

USE THIS WORKSHEET AS YOU LISTEN TO "GAINING A NEW ATTITUDE ON LIFE, PART 1."

Writer of letter on joy is _____, an unlikely source.

QUALITIES THAT CAN JUMP-START A LIFE

_____   What are you doing that makes God smile?

Philippians 1:11

_____   What are you doing that you are called to do?

Philippians 1:18

Philippians 1:21, 27

_____ What is one thing you are doing that will not fail?

Isaiah 55:10-11

Philippians 1:14

1 Corinthians 15:58

_____ What is one thing you are doing that will outlive you?

Philippians 2:4

Philippians 2:15-16

Set your _____ on pleasing God.

God has _____ that will not fail.

Anything you do _____ is not wasted, and it will _____.

Sometimes we are doing less than that which _____.

Consider your _____.

PART 2:
GOING DEEPER

PERSONAL STUDY AND REFLECTION

· What causes folks to get into a slump? What causes you to get into a
  slump?

_____

_____

_____

_____

_____

_____

_____

- *Philippians is a treatise on joy. We wonder how in the world a man who had every reason to complain finds so many reasons to rejoice. Paul lived a life of praise.*

- How did Paul have the ability to rejoice in such difficult circumstances?

_____

_____

_____

_____

_____

_____

_____

· You need a priority greater than this life. What is that priority?

_____

_____

_____

_____

_____

· You will _____ me how to _____ a holy life.

Being _____ you will _____ me with _____;

at your right hand I will find _____ forever.

Psalm 16:11

- What is the legacy you wish to leave?

_____

_____

_____

_____

_____

_____

_____

- *Be careful about that which you dream because dreams can come true. You need a priority that is greater than this life.*

· What quality in this lesson do you need to add to your life?

_____

_____

_____

_____

_____

_____

· List ways you intend to get out of a slump:

_____

_____

_____

- *It is hard to be discouraged when you are caught up in something that is going to last for eternity.*

- Are there any dreams in your life that need to change?

_____

_____

_____

_____

_____

_____

_____

Nothing can stop the man with the right mental attitude from achieving his goal; nothing on earth can help the man with the wrong mental attitude.

THOMAS JEFFERSON

LESSON TWO:

OVERCOMING A
BAD ATTITUDE

*In your lives you must think
and act like Christ Jesus.*

PHILIPPIANS 2:5

OVERVIEW

I love milk. I am a confessed milkaholic. One of the saddest days of my life was when I learned that whole milk was unhealthy. With great reluctance I have adapted to the watered-down version—but on occasion I still allow myself the hallowed ecstasy of a cold glass of whole milk and a hot, gooey, chocolate chip cookie.

In my years of appreciating the fine fruit of the cow I have learned that a high price is paid for leaving milk out of the refrigerator. Sweet milk turns sour from being too warm too long. Sweet dispositions turn sour for the same reason. Let aggravation stew without a period of cooling down, and the result? A bad, bitter, clabberish attitude.

The tenth chapter of Luke describes the step-by-step process of the sweet becoming sour.

It's the story of Martha. A dear soul given to hospitality and organization. More frugal than frivolous, more practical than pensive, her household is a tight ship and she is the stern captain. The problem is not Martha's choice to host. The problem is Martha's heart, a heart soured with anxiety. Bless her heart, Martha wanted to do right. But bless her heart, her heart was wrong. Her heart, Jesus said, was worried. As a result she turned from a happy servant into a beast of burden. She was worried: worried about cooking, worried about pleasing, worried about too much. So much so that she started bossing God around. Worry will do that to you. It makes you forget who's in charge.

It's easy to forget who is the servant and who is to be served. Satan knows that. This tool of distortion is one of Satan's slyest. Note: He didn't take Martha out of the kitchen; he took away her purpose in the kitchen. What matters more than the type of service is the heart behind the service. A bad attitude spoils the gift we leave on the altar for God. God is more pleased with the quiet attention of a sincere servant than the noisy service of a sour one.

Guard your attitude. God has gifted you with talents. He has done the same to your neighbor. If you concern yourself with your neighbor's talents, you will neglect yours. But if you concern yourself with yours, you could inspire both.

PART 1:
FOLLOW-ALONG NOTES

USE THIS WORKSHEET AS YOU LISTEN TO "GAINING A NEW ATTITUDE ON LIFE, PART 2."

- Luke 10:38-42 – Jesus Comes to Visit

- Differences in Martha and Mary

_____

_____

_____

_____

- God honors _____.

STEPS TO OVERCOME A BAD ATTITUDE

1._____ - take time to cool down

    Proverbs 29:11

    Proverbs 21:23

    Proverbs 13:3

    Proverbs 10:19

2. _____ - take time to slow down

    Luke 10:40-41

3. _____ - take time to look up

    Luke 10:42

PART 2:
GOING DEEPER

PERSONAL STUDY AND REFLECTION

• Take a personal inventory and decide if you are more likely to follow Mary
or Martha's example. What steps do you take to ensure that your focus
doesn't become stuck on yourself?

_____

_____

_____

_____

_____

_____

· **Read Luke 10:42.** What is this "one thing" the Lord is talking about to Martha?

_____

_____

_____

_____

· What is significant about the Lord's words, "Mary has chosen the better thing"? How does this comment relate to your own life?

_____

_____

_____

_____

- **Read Matthew 21:28-32.** What does this parable teach us about service? What lesson might Martha have learned from it?

_____

_____

_____

_____

- What point is Jesus making in verses 31-32? Why does he sound so harsh here?

_____

_____

_____

_____

- *Mary chose the better thing. She chose to sit at the feet of Christ.*

- Discuss the following statement: "God is more pleased with the quiet attention of a sincere servant than the noisy service of a sour one."

_____

_____

_____

_____

_____

_____

_____

_____

If we will be quiet and ready enough,
we shall find compensation in every disappointment.

HENRY DAVID THOREAU

LESSON THREE:

DEALING WITH DISAPPOINTMENT

Lord, hear my voice; listen to my prayer for help.

PSALM 130:2

OVERVIEW

Ten-year-old Phineas was up before the sun was. He'd scarcely slept
the night before. And long before a sound was heard in the house, he was
downstairs with his bag packed, ready to climb into the wagon.

The year was 1820. And Phineas was about to see an island. His island.
The island promised to him at birth. The day he was born, his grandfather
presented newborn Phineas with a deed, a sizable portion of Connecticut
land called Ivy Island. And today, for the first time, Phineas was to see it.

Not every boy is born a proprietor. Phineas's parents were always quick
to remind their son of this. They urged him not to forget them when he
came of age. Neighbors feared that the young landowner wouldn't want to
play with their children.

Their concerns were legitimate. Phineas was different from his
playmates. While they dreamed of dragons and knights, his fantasies were
of Ivy Island. Someday he would be lord of his own territory. He'd build a
house. Start a farm. Raise cattle. Rule his domain.

When you own an island you feel important.

When you own an island, you want to see it. Phineas had yet to see
his. He pleaded with his father to take him to the island and, finally, in the
summer of 1820, his father agreed.

Three sleepless nights preceded the expedition. Then, early that morning, Phineas, his father, and a hired hand climbed into the buggy and began the long-anticipated journey. Finally, Phineas would see his land.

He could scarcely sit still. At the top of each hill he would ask, "Are we nearly there? Can I see it from here?" And his father would encourage him to be patient and assure him that they were drawing near.

Finally, his dad pointed north beyond a meadow to a row of tall trees stretching into the sky.

"There, he said. "There is Ivy Island."

Phineas was overcome. He jumped from the wagon and dashed through the meadow, leaving his father far behind. He raced to the row of trees into an opening from which Ivy Island was visible.

When he saw the land he stopped. His heart sank.

Ivy Island was five acres of snake-infested marshland. His grandfather had called it the most valuable land in Connecticut. But it was worthless. His father had told him it was a generous gift. It wasn't. It was a joke . . . a cruel joke. As stunned Phineas stared, the father and the hired hand roared with laughter.

Phineas was not the fortunate beneficiary of the family. He was the laughingstock of the family. Grandfather Taylor had played a joke on his heir.

Phineas didn't laugh. Nor did he forget. That disappointment shaped his life. He, the deceived, made a lifestyle out of deception. The little boy fooled made a career out of fooling people.

You don't know him as Phineas. You know him as P.T. You don't know him as a landowner; you know him as a promoter. You know him as the one who coined the phrase, "There's a sucker born every minute." He spent his life proving it. Such was the life of P.T. Barnum.

And such is the life of many others, many others who have been told they'd be taken to the Promised Land only to find themselves taken to the swamp. Now they are faced with a decision. What do they do with their disillusionment? What do they do with their broken hearts?

PART 1:
FOLLOW-ALONG NOTES

Use this worksheet as you listen to "Gaining a New Attitude on Life, Part 3."

· Luke 24:13-35. The disappointment of the followers of Christ

JESUS UNDERSTANDS THAT
SOMETIMES WE DON'T UNDERSTAND

· Consequences of Disappointment –

Clouded _____ – Luke 24:15-16

Hardened _____ – Luke 24:22-24

· The Cause of Disappointment –

Unmet _____ –Luke 24:19-21

FAITH IS THE CONVICTION THAT GOD KNOWS MORE THAN WE DO ABOUT LIFE, AND HE WILL GET US THROUGH

- God's Cure for Disappointment –

  Honest Expectations

  Jesus tells _____ – Luke 24:27

- The cure for disappointment is to go back _____ .

PART 2:
GOING DEEPER

PERSONAL STUDY AND REFLECTION

- Try to recall the first time you were heartbroken. How did you respond? How long did it take you to recover? What did friends or family do to help you recover?

_____

_____

_____

_____

_____

- In what ways does despair harden our hearts and make us cynical and calloused? Why is this dangerous?

_____

_____

_____

_____

_____

_____

_____

_____

- How can the knowledge that God is still in control affect our outlook when our heart is broken?

_____

_____

_____

_____

_____

_____

_____

_____

_____

· Notice the statement from Cleopas in Luke 24:21, "... but we were hoping."
How does this phrase sum up his deep heartbreak?

_____

_____

_____

_____

_____

_____

_____

_____

- **Read Psalm 135:5-14.** What picture of God do you receive from this
  Scripture? How do these pictures help us in times of heartbreak?

_____

_____

_____

_____

_____

_____

_____

_____

_____

- **Read Daniel 4:34-35.** Share ways this passage will give comfort to the heartbroken.

_____

_____

_____

_____

_____

_____

_____

_____

The Bible has many references to anger and bitterness. Read the following Scriptures and list a principle you need to take away from each specific verse. It may also be helpful to memorize the Scripture to use when the moment arises that may cause you to harbor anger or bitterness.

Psalm 103:8 _____   1 Corinthians 13:5 _____

Ephesians 4:26 _____   Psalm 145:8 _____

Numbers 24:10 _____   Proverbs 29:8 _____

Psalm 86:15 _____   1 Timothy 2:8 _____

Joel 2:13 _____   Psalm 78:38 _____

Colossians 3:8 _____   James 1:20 _____

Proverbs 15:1 _____   Psalm 4:4 _____ ∎

He that cannot forgive others,
breaks the bridge over which he himself
must pass if he would ever reach heaven;
for everyone has need to be forgiven.

LORD HERBERT

LESSON FOUR:

DON'T MISS THE PARTY

Do not be bitter or angry or mad.
Be kind and loving to each other,
and forgive each other just
as God forgave you in Christ.

EPHISIANS 4:31-32

OVERVIEW

The case of the elder brother. A difficult one because he looked so good. He kept his room straight and his nose clean. He played by the rules and paid all his dues. His resume? Impeccable. His credit? Squeaky clean. And loyalty? While his brother was sowing wild oats, he stayed home and sowed the crops. On the outside he was everything a father could want in a son. But on the inside he was sour and hollow. Overcome by jealousy. Consumed by anger. Blinded by bitterness.

You remember the story. It's perhaps the best known of all the parables Jesus told. It is the story of the lost son—the boy who broke his father's heart by taking his inheritance and taking off. He traded his dignity for a whisky bottle and his self-respect for a pigpen. Then comes the son's sorrow and his decision to go home. He hopes his dad will give him a job on the farm and an apartment over the garage. What he finds is a father who has kept his absent son's place set at the table and the porch light on every night.

The father is so excited to see his son, you'll never guess what he does. That's right! He throws a party! We party-loving prodigals love what he did, but it infuriated the elder brother. It's not hard to see why. "So, is this how a guy gets recognition in this family? Get drunk and go broke and you get a party?" So the older brother sat outside the house and pouted. He felt he was a victim of inequity. When the father came out to meet him, the son started at the top, listing the atrocities of his life. To hear him say it, his woes began the day he was born.

It appears that both sons spent time in the pigpen. One in the pen of rebellion—the other in the pen of self-pity. The younger one has come home. The older one hasn't. He's still in the slop. The brother was bitter because he focused on what he didn't have and forgot what he did have. His father reminded him—and us—that he had everything he'd always had. He had his job, his place, his name, and his inheritance. The only thing he didn't have was the spotlight. And because he wasn't content to share it—he missed the party.

PART 1:
FOLLOW-ALONG NOTES

USE THIS WORKSHEET AS YOU LISTEN TO "GAINING A NEW ATTITUDE ON LIFE, PART 4."

- A Father Throws A Party – Luke 15:25-32

Definition of Bitterness _____

_____

THE ELDER SON'S ATTITUDE

Claimed to be in _____ (seed of bitterness)

Claimed to be _____ and _____

Tools to a bitter heart: _____ and _____

Claimed to be _____ (vs.30)

THE DUNGEON OF BITTERNESS

Who is a candidate?

THE FATHER'S RESPONSE

The Father showed incredible _____.

THE PRESCRIPTION FOR BITTERNESS

God invites us to sit at the feast.

Hebrews 12:15

You need to know your _____.

You need to know the _____ of the kingdom of heaven.

PART 2:
GOING DEEPER

PERSONAL STUDY AND REFLECTION

· Give your own definition of *bitterness*.

_____

_____

_____

· Discuss the high expectations the elder son had for his world. Why were they so unrealistic?

_____

_____

_____

• Why don't some people "come and join the party"? What reasons to they give?

_____

_____

_____

_____

_____

• Where _____ and _____ are, there will be

confusion and every kind of _____. But the _____

that comes from _____ is first of all _____, then _____,

gentle, and easy to please. This wisdom is always ready to _____ those

who are _____ and to do _____ for others. James 3:16-17

- In Luke 15:21 how did the father react to the younger son's speech? What might it suggest to you about your own prayer life?

_____

_____

_____

_____

_____

_____

_____

- *The elder brother was angry at the reception that the father gave the younger brother. He claimed to be blameless, betrayed, and better than the younger brother.*

· With whom do you most identify in this story? The older son? The younger son? The father?

_____

_____

_____

_____

· **Read Hebrews 12:14-15.** What connection is there in verse 14 between living in peace with all people and being holy? Which one logically comes first?

_____

_____

_____

_____

• In what ways does the story of Luke 15:11-32 illustrate the truths of
Hebrews 12:14-15?

_____

_____

_____

_____

_____

_____

_____

_____ ■

PROMISES FROM GAINING A NEW ATTITUDE ON LIFE

Savor the following promises that God gives to those who determine to embrace a new attitude. One way that you can carry the message of this study with you everywhere in your heart is through the lost art of Scripture memorization. Select a few of the verses below to commit to memory.

I said to the LORD, "You are my Lord.
Every good thing I have comes from you."

PSALM 16:2

Live a life of love just as Christ loved us and gave himself
for us as a sweet-smelling offering and sacrifice to God.

EPHESIANS 5:2

Be full of joy in the Lord always. I will say again, be full of joy.

PHILIPPIANS 4:4

Let us live in a right way, like people who belong to the day.

ROMANS 13:13

God, you do what is right. You know our thoughts and feelings.

PSALM 7:9

So I tell you: Live by following the Spirit.
Then you will not do what your sinful selves want.

GALATIANS 5:16

Do not be bitter or angry or mad.
Never shout angrily or say things to hurt others.
Never do anything evil.
Be kind and loving to each other, and forgive
each other just as God forgave you in Christ.

EPHESIANS 4:31-32

People who work for peace in a peaceful way
plant a good crop of right-living.

JAMES 4:18

Don't ever forget my words; keep them always in mind.
They are the key to life for those who find them;
they bring health to the whole body.

PROVERBS 4:22-21

SUGGESTIONS FOR MEMBERS OF A GROUP STUDY

The Bible says that we should not forsake the assembling of ourselves together (see Hebrews 10:25). A small-group Bible study is one of the best ways to grow in your faith. As you meet together with other people, you will discover new truths about God's Word and challenge one another to greater levels of faith. The following are suggestions for you to get the most out of a small-group study of this material.

1. Come to the study prepared. Follow the suggestions for individual study mentioned previously. You will find that careful preparation will greatly enrich your time spent in group discussion.

2. Be willing to participate in the discussion. The leader of your group will not be lecturing. Instead, he or she will be encouraging the members of the group to discuss what they have learned. The leader will be asking the questions that are found in this guide.

3. Stick to the topic being discussed.

4. Be sensitive to the other members of the group. Listen attentively when they describe what they have learned. You may be surprised by their insights! Many questions do not have "right" answers, particularly questions that aim at meaning or application. Instead the questions push us to explore the passage more thoroughly.

5. When possible, link what you say to the comments of others. Also be affirming whenever you can. This will encourage some of the more hesitant members of the group to participate.

6. Expect God to teach you through the passage being discussed and through the other members of the group. Pray that you will have an enjoyable and profitable time together, but also that as a result of this study, you will find ways that you can take action individually and/or as a group.

7. Remember that anything said in the group is considered confidential and should not be discussed outside the group unless specific permission is given to do so.

LEADER'S GUIDE

LESSON ONE: HOW TO GET OUT OF A SLUMP

1. Begin the session with prayer. Ask God to be with you as you begin to study his Word together.

2. Play the audio segment of the CD entitled "Gaining a New Attitude on Life, Part 1." Encourage group members to take notes in the section of their study guide entitled "Follow-Along Notes."

3. Begin group discussion by asking the following questions. Allow each group member ample time to answer, if they desire to do so.

   - How can the attitude of Paul be an example to all believers?

   - As we try to get to where we are going, in what ways do we need to consider where we might end up?

   - What priorities do you feel a follower of Christ should demonstrate?

   - What attitude should you have when service in God's kingdom shows no fruit? Share some ways to gain that attitude.

- As you work to get out of a slump, what obstacle is the greatest?

4. Remind everyone to complete the "Going Deeper: Personal Study and Reflection" section for lesson two before the next group session.

5. Be sure to close in prayer. Invite the group participants to share prayer requests with the group and encourage them to pray for one another.

LESSON TWO: OVERCOMING A BAD ATTITUDE

1. Begin the session with prayer. Ask God to be with you as you begin to study his Word together.

2. Play the audio segment of the CD entitled "Gaining a New Attitude on Life, Part 2." Encourage group members to take notes in the section of their study guide entitled "Follow-Along Notes."

3. Begin group discussion by asking the following questions. Allow each group member ample time to answer, if they desire to do so.

- Share your attitude about the story of Martha and Mary. Based on this study is there a certain point you find more personal?

- Why do you think Martha only complained about Mary not helping?

- Of the three ways to overcome a bad attitude, which one is the most difficult?

- Share some benefits of overcoming a bad attitude.

- As you reflect on times you struggled with a bad attitude, do you see a pattern in what created that attitude? What can you do to avoid that pattern?

4. Remind everyone to complete the "Going Deeper: Personal Study and Reflection" section for lesson three before the next group session.

5. Be sure to close in prayer. Invite the group participants to share prayer requests with the group and encourage them to pray for one another.

LESSON THREE: DEALING WITH DISAPPOINTMENT

1. Begin the session with prayer. Ask God to be with you as you begin to study his Word together.

2. Play the audio segment of the CD entitled "Gaining a New Attitude on Life, Part 3." Encourage group members to take notes in the section of their study guide entitled "Follow-Along Notes."

3. Begin group discussion by asking the following questions. Allow each group member ample time to answer, if they desire to do so.

- Place yourself on the road that day with the followers of Christ. What would be your points of discussion?

- List some dangers of clouded vision as it relates to disappointment.

- Share ways to soften a hardened heart damaged by disappointment.

- What strength do you gain from reading the story Jesus shared with the men in Luke 24:27?

- Compare the response to disappointment when faith is present and when faith is absent.

4. Remind everyone to complete the "Going Deeper: Personal Study and Reflection" section for lesson four before the next group session.

5. Be sure to close in prayer. Invite the group participants to share prayer requests with the group and encourage them to pray for one another.

LESSON FOUR: DON'T MISS THE PARTY

1. Begin the session with prayer. Ask God to be with you as you begin to study his Word together.

2. Play the audio segment of the CD entitled "Gaining a New Attitude on Life, Part 4." Encourage group members to take notes in the section of their study guide entitled "Follow-Along Notes."

3. Begin group discussion by asking the following questions. Allow each group member ample time to answer, if they desire to do so.

   - In the story of the prodigal son, have you given much thought to the response of the older brother? How do we relate to the brother's attitude?

   - How do you explain the response of the father to his prodigal son and to the older brother?

   - What do you feel causes bitterness? List some ways to avoid going to the dungeon of bitterness.

   - Read Hebrews 12:14-15. In light of this Scripture, how should we deal with bitterness?

4. Be sure to close in prayer. Invite the group participants to share prayer requests with the group and encourage them to pray for one another.

MAX LUCADO'S

MAX on life

S E R I E S

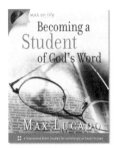

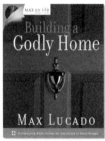

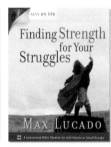

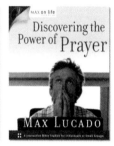

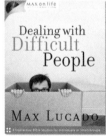

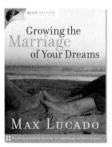

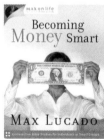